4 / 4 / 90

Thank you so much
for coming and sharing
with us.

Merlissie Middleton

THE BLACK CHURCH
VS.
THE SYSTEM

THE BLACK CHURCH VS. THE SYSTEM

MERLISSIE ROSS MIDDLETON

VANTAGE PRESS
New York   Washington   Atlanta   Hollywood

FIRST EDITION

Copyright © 1976 by Merlissie Ross Middleton

Published by Vantage Press, Inc.
516 West 34th Street, New York, New York 10001

Manufactured in the United States of America
Standard Book Number 533-02289-4

DEDICATED

TO

the memory of my late
husband,
John A. Middleton,
my son,
Phillip Middleton,
and my daughters,
Ann Faye Reed
and
Johnsy A. Middleton

ACKNOWLEDGMENTS

The writer of this book is appreciative of the contributions others have made to its successful conclusion. Especially does the writer wish to express gratitude to Dr. Hylan Lewis for his unfailing patience, wise guidance and sympathetic encouragement; the late Dr. Mozell Hill, Dr. Albert N. Whiting and others of the Atlanta University Faculty for their inspiration and challenge to scholarly research; the Reverend Homer C. McEwen and the late Mrs. J. B. Greenwood for assistance in tracing down and obtaining hard-to-get and valuable materials and journals; Dr. Benjamin E. Mays for writing the foreword; and Morris Brown College and Mr. Norris B. Herndon for assistance in publishing this book.

CONTENTS

LIST OF TABLES

LIST OF FIGURES

FOREWORD

The black church is perhaps the most significant institution that black people own and control. Its contribution to the total life of America is most outstanding.

Despite this fact, the black church has not received the serious attention of scholars that it deserves. Only a few books have been written in an attempt to appraise in depth the contribution the black church has made to American life. Several local books have been written about the black church and a few on a larger dimension such as *The Negro Church* by W. E. B. DuBois; *The History of the Negro Church* by Carter G. Woodson; and *The Negro Church in America* by E. Franklin Frazier. *The Negro's Church* by Benjamin E. Mays and Joseph Nicholson, published in 1933, was the most comprehensive study based on wide research that had been made up to that time and there has been nothing comparable since.

Though a local study, *The Black Church vs. The System* has national significance because the problems confronting the First Congregational Church in Atlanta are typical of what black churches face throughout the nation.

Within recent years more trained blacks are qualifying for pastoral work. *The Black Church vs. The System* presents a challenge to church leadership to meet the problems presented in its pages. The author has written a volume that will be used in sociological and religious circles for many years to come.

BENJAMIN E. MAYS

THE BLACK CHURCH
VS.
THE SYSTEM

CHAPTER I

INTRODUCTION

THE CHURCH AND THE COMMUNITY

The evolution of the city with its consequent redistribution of peoples both in terms of social role and status and physical location has great significance for the institutions which organize life. They are profoundly affected by the social and ecological processes of the urban area. For example, in the case of the urban church, it has been observed that:

The city church, like other forms of social organization, bears the imprint of its environment. First, there is a tendency towards specialization and departmentalization. The multiplicity of divergent denominations in the city, and the increasing division of labor within the church itself, are indications of this trend. Second, the church shows a tendency toward a cooperativeness that is characteristic of other forms of social organization. Although there are still innumerable ritualistic and credal differences between religious groups, many of the sectarian barriers which at one period of their natural history almost completely isolated the churches from one another have been modified by the socializing effect of urban life. Finally social stratification in the city is reflected in the structure and functions of the worship, social and religious values of the groups, and relations with other organizations in the community.[1]

It is a matter of common observation that church edifices representing denominations known to be wealthy are frequently found in upper-class residential areas, just as it is known that "store front" churches are located in disorganized neighborhoods.[2]

In a study made in the 1920s, ten urban types of Protestant churches resulting from city evolution were distinguished; and it was concluded that churches "tend largely to reflect the economic neighborhoods to which they minister."[3]

Although it is probably true that churches tend to reflect the status of the neighborhoods in which they are located, it is also true that churches show different degrees of adaptation to the city as measured by the type of neighborhood in which they are located and the geographical areas and social strata from which they draw their members. It is probably true that people tend to be more spatially mobile than the physical structures of many of their institutions such as churches and schools.

Drake and Cayton, in a study of churches in the Chicago Negro community, after indicating a relationship between status and denominational affiliations, noted an instance of a marooned high-status church:

One Baptist church and one Methodist Episcopal church, as well as two A.M.E. churches are considered high-status, but not upper class though they have quite a few upper class members, including several manufacturers and two former bankers. The pastors of the upper class churches are all college-trained men devoid of the crude emotional tricks common in many other churches. Upper class church buildings tend to be small, but are very well cared for and artistically decorated. Two of the churches are situated in higher-status residential neighborhoods, but have not adapted their

2

program to the community, preferring to draw higher status members from a distance.[4]

This project is undertaken to describe the residential distribution and mobility of the membership of a high-status church which is apparently marooned in a low-status neighborhood; this church draws a significant proportion of its members from more distant and higher status communities.[5] The church chosen is a well-known Atlanta church, located near the heart of the city in one of the oldest Negro residential districts. The following section is devoted to a brief summary of the church's history and an indication of its relationship to the Atlanta community.

History of First Congregational Church

First Church, located on the northeast corner of Houston and Courtland Streets in downtown Atlanta, was founded in 1867—just after the close of the Civil War—and rebuilt in 1908. The side wall that faced Ellis Street in the 1867 structure was retained in the 1908 structure. The church was started as a mission in Storrs School on May 26, 1867, by the Reverend Frederick Ayers and his wife, of Wisconsin. In it was housed the Ralph Minor Institute, which featured a cooking program, a gymnasium, and a library. Out of the Ralph Minor Institute of Storrs School grew Atlanta University.

An old member recalls:

Everything happened right in this neighborhood. Our church was an institutional church. There was the Ralph Minor Institute with a cooking school, gymnasium, and library. The parsonage was next door. There was a working girl's home at 185 Courtland that started in 1913. It was the first of its kind in Atlanta—a place for girls to live that came here to work. Storrs School worshipped in a tent during the erection of the

3

new church. People and members lived right here on Piedmont. Three presidents of the United States have visited our church. We stood on the steps of the church and sang, "Let Us Cheer The Weary Traveler" when President Taft visited us. Presidents Coolidge and Roosevelt have both been to our church.

Among the original members of First Church were Frederick Ayers, a missionary from Wisconsin who started the first mission at First Church in connection with Storrs School; Elizabeth Ayers, the wife of Frederick Ayers and also a missionary from Wisconsin; Edmund A. Ware, first president and founder of Atlanta University; Charles A. Morgan, a groceryman with a store on the corner of Auburn and Butler, whose grandchildren still worship at First Church; Mrs. Anna Morgan, wife of Charles A. Morgan, and a housekeeper; Jacob B. Miller, a charter member of the church and a cabinetmaker; Stephen Berry, a charter member; Robert Johnson, a charter member; Mrs. Celia Graves, a housekeeper; and Abraham Farrar, a charter member who "had a bass voice and was a choir member."[6]

The pastors of First Church during its one hundred and nine years have been the Reverends Cyrus W. Francis, Edward C. Rogers, Charles M. Southgate, Simon Ashley, Charles W. Hawley, Evart E. Kent, Samuel H. Robinson, Henry H. Proctor, Russell Brown, William Faulkner, Clarence Wright, and Homer C. McEwen. Seven of the twelve ministers of First Church were white persons who were closely associated with Atlanta University. The church is now being pastored by its fifth Negro minister.

Community Setting

First Church, when founded, was a part of a neighborhood that was considered "a better residential area" by contemporaries. In two generations, this neighborhood has changed in function, population, and physical character. The church is now in a neighborhood of service stations, warehouses, truck garages, and factories. Dwellings that at one time accommodated single families have been converted into multiple dwellings, housing several families of the lower-income group. Former dwellings are now being used to house such agencies as the Gate City Day Nursery and the Working Girl's Home. In many instances, residences have been completely replaced by service stations, factories, and truck garages. This community exhibits most of the characteristics of what Burgess calls the "area in transition."

The zone surrounding the central business district has been designated as the area of transition, because it is in the immediate path of business and industrial expansion, and has an empheral character. Unlike the business district, which is non-residential for the most part, the zone in transition tends to be heavily populated by the lower income classes, by Old World immigrants, and by rural migrants, by unconventional folk and by social outcasts, such as criminals and prostitutes.[7]

In the neighborhood of the church today, one finds, on the same side of the street, C. C. Wilson Wholesale Grocers, Chandler Machinery Company, one residential dwelling, the Cathcart Allied Storage Company, the Southern Printing Company, a private parking lot for the customers of the Southern Poster Printing Company, the Mutual Supply Company, and a service station. Across the street, on Houston between Courtland and Piedmont, one finds a parking lot directly in front of the church. Going toward Piedmont Street, one finds the Sign-Craft Company, the Johnson Battery Company, a parking lot for the vans of the Cathcart Allied Storage Company, a dilapidated house with a "for sale" sign on it, the Chas. N. Walker Roofing Company, and a hotel on the corner of Piedmont and Houston.

At the corner of Courtland and Houston (across the street), one finds two service stations. On Courtland, across the street from the church and between Houston and Ellis Streets, there are two more service stations and the Atlanta Glass Company. Behind the church, on Courtland, are two residential dwellings, a parking lot, and a service station. On the corner of Ellis and Courtland, there is a liquor store.

If one should continue on Houston Street across Courtland for two blocks, one would be in the downtown section of Atlanta, where we find the Cypress Hotel, the Hotel Hampton, the Davis Restaurant, the Fulton Bank, a Western Union Office, and other downtown businesses.

The commercial and transitorial character of the neighborhood in which the church is located is emphasized by the fact that there are but a few residential dwellings in the immediate vicinity.

First Church is located on the western edge of census tract F–28. Census Tract F–27, which adjoins tract F–28, incorporates a good slice of the main downtown business district and, except for commercial hotels, it is a nonresidential area. Census tract data for tracts F–27, F–28, and F–29 give important statistical indices to the blighted character of the church's neighborhood. The following facts about tract F–28, based upon the 1940 census figures, seem pertinent:

Of the total population of 9,767, ninety-nine percent (9,712) were Negroes. Fifty-six percent of the Negro population was female.

Of the 2,246 persons employed, fifty-eight percent were domestic service and other service workers; ten percent laborers; and five percent professional workers.

The median monthly rent was $10.60.

Of the 2,869 dwelling units reporting, slightly less

6

than one in five (18 percent) were one-family dwellings.

Of 2,286 units for which data were available, two-thirds (66.0 percent) were in need of major repairs; nearly forty percent had no running water; and one-sixth (12.2 percent) had no flush toilets.[8]

There is much objective evidence for the fact that First Church is now located in an area of physical blight, deterioration, and significant disorganization as measured by land use, housing, health, and crime data. In a recent statistical description of the Atlanta area, tracts F–27, F–28, and F–29 have ranked among the highest in the incidence of death, sickness, illegitimacy, crime, and vice.[9]

Impact on Community

First Church received national attention for the role it played during and after the 1906 Atlanta race riot. A pamphlet printed in Boston in 1914 refers to First Church as "the church that saved a city."

Bruce Barton, its author, wrote:

The mob did terrible things on those three days. Where the railroad runs under the street, on the high bridge, they caught a shuddering colored boy. No one in the crowd knew him; he had nothing to do with the riot, but he was colored and that was enough. Before he realized it they had closed in solidly about him, breathing forth their threats and aiming their blows at his face. For a moment he glanced wildly about for an avenue of escape, and finding none, leaped over the iron railing and threw himself on the tracks below. He died an hour later.

On one of the main streets two colored boys ran a bootblack parlor and were busy at their work when the mob rushed by. Someone shouted; the crowd hesitated, saw the boys at work and, too eager to wait for the door, crashed into the little shop through the plate glass window. Terrified, the two scampered into the farthest corner of the room and waited there, trembling. And at that moment a soldier, whose shoes they had been shining, leaped down from the chair and, brandishing his cane, defied them all. "Back," he shouted, "any of you that touches those boys will have to fight me first! I'll brain the first one that takes a step forward!"

They looked at him, eyes flashing with righteous anger, his cane swung in a muscular grip, and then, one by one, they slunk through the door into the street. So two lives that might have been added to the wreckage were saved. . . .

. . . Enough destruction was achieved to leave its eternal mark upon the glory of the city and to plunge a portion of the population, at least, into complete despair. There were 51,902 Negroes in Atlanta, over one-third of all the people in the city. . . .

. . . After two or three days the terror died on the street, but it raged still in the hearts of the people. And particularly of that first class of the colored folk, who had come out of the country to make their homes in Atlanta and to acquire money to educate their children and be a credit to their kind. "We shall have to move," they said to one another, repeating it over like frightened children. "There will be no opportunity for us in Atlanta from now on; the disease is checked, but there remains the wound, ugly, glaring, a bitter reminder forever that we are different, that we are set behind the veil, that we may go thus far and no farther. Whatever we have gathered together here that cannot go must be sacrificed, for we must seek out a new city where there is no scar."

So the comment ran, and all over the city—that is, the colored city of 51,902 with which the story deals—men began trembling to gather their goods about them preparatory to flight. For a few hours a whole city of 51,902 souls hung in the balance. One day it was there, prosperous, contented, aspiring; and the next day it shuddered on the brink of oblivion.[10]

Evaluating the role the church played in the Atlanta riot, Barton states that the great towering figure of

Henry H. Proctor of the First Congregational Church, colored, in Atlanta, who was a graduate of Yale and the successor to two white preachers, played a role that Atlanta could not forget. Proctor went from one businessman to another telling them that this is not the time to leave Atlanta, but rather to take advantage of the opportunity the riot had given. Proctor felt that out of the riot should come a better understanding between the races and that there should be glorious progress for his people.

He consoled a grief-stricken man by saying:

Now's our chance to show them the stuff we're made of—that we are real men, not grown-up children as they want us to believe. Let's show them the men we are. Let's begin by erecting a church as has never been erected by colored men before, an institutional church embodying all that is modern and approved in church work. Let that be our answer to the riot; let's begin now.

As a result of the moving spirit of Henry H. Proctor, the colored city of Atlanta, 51,902 souls, found themselves building that church.

They were determined to show the white city the substance of their soul.

According to Bruce Barton, First Congregational Church is the only church that he has knowledge of that has the right to claim that it saved a city.

He narrates his conversation with one of the successful members of the community who told him that he came to Atlanta as a raw boy fresh from the farm and went to First Church. As a result of the inspiration gained, he remained, as he said, "I'm going to attend this church and I'm going to amount to something in this city." Today his name is on the door of the only Negro bank in the city, where he is director. The Negro bank is officered by two prominent men in the church.

First Congregational Church is comprised of members in a wide sphere of the social and political spectrum of the city.

It was emphatically explained by Barton in his comments:

Many city churches I have seen whose pastors could name over to me prominent and wealthy men among their members, or the husbands of their members. But I do not know where else there is a church that seems so thoroughly to have permeated the life of the city—its own particular city—as has this First Congregational church in Atlanta. For a whole day I went back and forth in its city and up and down in it. The largest Negro printing establishment is owned by one of its members, and the only Negro newspaper is edited by him. The oldest drug store in the city, the one singled out by the government to be a sub-postal station, is presided over by one of the church's staunch supporters. I talked with a church trustee, a grocer who in his forty years and more of active business life has gathered a clientele more largely white than colored and accumulated a fortune of more than 40,000 dollars. Stationery stores, tailoring establishments, theaters, meat markets, photograph galleries of particular merit—each bore upon its face the name of a member of First Church.[11]

Out of the race riot also grew the Atlanta Interracial Committee that has had as its purpose the seeking of a better understanding between the races.

The National Medical Association, now recognized as one of America's outstanding professional and learned societies, had its beginning among Atlanta medics, and under the inspiration and leadership of First Church.

The first public library for the use of the Negroes of Atlanta was started at First Church.

The first organized program of social service for Negro people in Atlanta was that of First Church.

The National Convention of Congregational Workers, for colored people, had its origin in First Church under the leadership of its first Negro pastor.

The pastors of First Church have traditionally been civic and welfare leaders. Pastors of First Church have served on the following: Board of Directors and Executive Commitee, Atlanta Branch, National Association for the Advancement of Colored People; Executive Committee of the Atlanta Urban League; the Board of Management of the Butler Street Y.M.C.A., Atlanta; Advisory Committee, Fulton and Dekalb County Child Welfare Association; Board of Directors, Carrie Steele Logan Home for Orphans; Troop Committees of Troops 90 and 140, Atlanta Council, Boy Scouts of America; Board of Directors and Executive Committee, Atlanta Civic and Political League; Negro State Planning Committee; State Interracial Commission; State Advisory Committee, Federal Forums; and Atlanta Vocational Guidance Council.

The Boy Scout movement was made available to colored boys through First Church under the pastorate of its third Negro pastor in 1931. The first colored troop to be chartered in Atlanta started out with thirty boys. This troop is still in existence, and members have won every honor in scouting; they include four Eagle Scouts, and the induction of their former scoutmaster, now a Scout commissioner, into the "Order of the Silver Eagle," the highest award in Scouting. There are now twenty-one Negro troops in the Atlanta Council, with an enrollment of over 350 boys; ninety-five Scout committeemen and adult leaders; and a District Committee of around thirty men, headed by the chairman of the Board of Deacons of First Church.

An organization known as the "Scout Mothers," to cooperate with scoutmasters and committeemen in furthering the development and welfare of the troops, was started in connection with Troop 90 of First Church; and it has been copied by other troops.

The pastor of First Church states its goal as the

11

broadening and deepening of religious experience through effectively organized and directed service. The church school is divided into kindergarten, primary, intermediate, junior, and senior departments. It provides religious training for the youth and adults of the church and community. The senior and junior choirs offer an opportunity for musical expression.

The church is used regularly each Sunday for Sunday School and church services. It is also the meeting place each Sunday for the Pilgrim Fellowship, which is a youth organization. These words appear on the church entrance, "Come In and Rest." The church is open, it is warm, and there is full-time janitorial service to aid in providing comfort for persons desiring to rest. It is used for meetings on the average of twenty to thirty times per month.

The Deacon's Parish is subdivided into nine groups, over each of which is placed a deacon, a deaconess, and a trustee; they assist the minister in looking after the spiritual needs of the members and the temporal interests of the church.

The Women's Missionary Society serves a religious as well as a social function. It gives the women of the church an opportunity to come together and fellowship as well as to plan and work out programs that are educational and inspirational. Their program includes local as well as foreign interests. The Deaconess Board works to keep alive the spiritual life and interest of the members. The social club has an interest in the social activities. The Servèttes is an organization of young unmarried women and matrons. They have a program designed to meet the needs of that group of women.

The foregoing activities indicate that First Church has from the beginning been one of the central places in the Negro community for educational, fraternal, civic, and community gatherings. Many local, state, and national movements for the social, economic, and educational advancement of the Negro people had their origin in this church. Many of the local organizations are very largely directed by First Church members who hold strategic places.

THE PROBLEM, THE DATA, AND THE METHOD

The specific purpose of this investigation is to describe and analyze the residential distribution of members of this church over a period of forty years in order to indicate (1) the changes in the spatial distribution of church members; (2) the types of residential movements; and (3) the extent of movement. The basic assumption underlying this study is that the spatial redistribution of members of this church has been a reflection of the growth and expansion of the Negro community with its consequent increase in occupational differentiation and pressure for new and better physical locations. Among the hypotheses guiding the collection of data and their analysis are these: (1) the percentage of members living in the immediate vicinity of First Church has consistently declined, in keeping with the changing social and economic characteristics of the area; (2) the current membership of First Church is dispersed over a significantly wider area than the earlier membership; and (3) a significant proportion of the membership of First Church lives in residential districts that are rated high by objective indices and community consensus.

In order to throw light on these hypotheses, the selective characteristics of membership for successive ten-year periods beginning in 1910 have been examined. The basic data, consisting of church records and membership rolls, are not available for the period prior to 1910. The following specific information was coded from these church records for the indicated periods: name of member, sex, and address were obtained from the records. Many of the names recurred one or more times in the records for the successive periods. It was possible to compare residential location for the respective periods and to calculate distances moved and to rate areas moved to. The data on membership and residence for the different periods were supplemented by documentary materials on the church, and interviews with the pastor, officers, and members of the church, particularly more elderly members whose association with the church has spanned many years.

These data were related to historical and demographic material on Atlanta. Extensive use was made of census tract data for 1930, 1940, and 1950, and a rating scale of residential areas developed by the Department of Sociology of Atlanta University.[12]

Three-by-five index cards were used to record the name, address, and the census tract number of each member during each of the years under review. The area rating was added to the 1950 cards. To facilitate organization and analysis, a color code was used for each of the periods. The corners of membership cards for 1910 were colored orange; 1920, red; 1930, white; 1940, green; and 1950, purple. Tabulations and summary tables were made showing the distribution of members by census tracts during each period.

Appropriate data were inserted on census tract maps for the respective periods. Names and addresses occurring in successive periods were separated and examined for residential movement. The former residence and the place moved to was tabulated and, with the aid of a scaled map, the distance in miles or fractions thereof was calculated. The areas moved to and the distances traveled were tabulated and compared for the respective periods.

Maps were made depicting the distances and directions moved by those who changed their residences over the respective ten-year periods.

RELATED LITERATURE

H. Paul Douglass, in *1,000 City Churches*, had a concern for the differences in the directional distribution of the members. He drew a parish map for 154 churches and showed the proportion of members living in the four sectors corresponding to the directions north, south, east, and west. With reference to the relationship between the church and local environment, he made this observation:

Starting with the center of a typical American city, one finds the downtown church. Working out from this center, one comes upon an ugly belt of territory characterized by less desirable habitations, especially boarding and rooming houses and frequently representing an old residential neighborhood that has seen better days. Here, crowded upon by industry and second-rate business, one finds the "near-downtown" church. Passing this zone by way of the avenues, one comes upon the high class residential districts with their family churches. Off the side streets one glimpses the working class churches. Down in the hollow by the railroad tracks are the foreign and the Negro churches, and still further out the rural churches. . . . He distinguishes ten urban types of Protestant churches. . . .[13]

In another study by Paul H. Douglass reported in 1950, he points out that:

Of 1350 metropolitan churches reported, 53 per cent have compact parishes in the sense that two-thirds or more of their people live within a mile of the church. About one-fifth have scattered parishes in the sense that less than one-third live within a mile of the church, the rest being widely dispersed.

The remainder of the churches show a moderate dispersal of constituents, from one-third to two-thirds living within a mile of the church. Suburbs show the smallest proportion of scattered or ravelled out parishes because population is sti

focusing upon them and they have not yet become centers of dispersal.

The majority of scattered parishes belong to churches located at or near city centers, from which the characteristic movement of population spurred by physical deterioration is continuously evicting people.

In rural areas, obviously, the distribution of constituents is a reflection of density of population. Open country people necessarily come considerable distances to church. Hamlet churches, however, in the open country frequently have exceedingly compact parishes and little rural out-reach.

Central location is naturally and properly sought by small denominations which have few constituents anywhere, and can most effectively bring them together at points where transit facilities focus and population is most accustomed to gather.[14]

This study stresses again that movements that are spurred by physical deterioration are continuously evicting people, and that central location is sought where transportation is convenient and population is accustomed to gather.

Wilson and Kolb conclude that:

Every society, and each of its component social systems, must put the land at its disposal to various uses (always including subsistence and habitation). But once the problem of sheer biological existence is solved (and very often before it is solved), the use of the land which shall predominate depends upon the way the society ranks its various goals and activities. Where religious values predominate, religious systems will preempt the most desirable land, and the other social systems must perforce adapt themselves accordingly. In a militaristic society, the use of the land will be primarily determined by the needs of war-making.[15]

Wilson and Kolb think that the value system of a society will determine the institution that will use the most desirable land.

Everett C. Hughes makes this observation about institutions:

The existence of the local units of an institution depends upon the continued presence of a population which will support them. A sharp decline in rates of reproduction will, in the absence of immigration, threaten certain institutions. Decline of the basic institutions may deprive the community of the means of supporting its service institutions. In our mobile world a population of one set of economic and cultural standards is often succeeded by another. In a community where this is in course of happening, churches, societies, and lodges, perhaps even restaurants and theatres may disappear. For while the newcomers may be religious, they often do not want the religious institutions of their predecessors. They are sociable, but within the framework of their own culture. They eat and amuse themselves, but may prefer spaghetti and Verdi to roast beef and Gilbert and Sullivan. While most institutions may adapt themselves to succession, less secular institutions can not. Succession itself is often the result of change in basic institutions; it is, in turn, change in many of the service institutions. If one were to discover which institutions do not change following such a succession of population he would have found an objective common denominator of our culture.[16]

When districts cease to be solid residential neighborhoods and become rooming house areas, slums, or foreign colonies the existing churches may survive by becoming missions, settlement houses, or club houses of the Y.M.C.A. type. In that case, they are generally supported by philanthropic gifts or by the mission funds of central denomination bodies rather than by the people who patronize them. One may advance the hypothesis that increase in mobility and in the intensity of sectarian spirit of the population of a community all tend to make the continued existence of local churches precarious.[17]

Hughes is of the opinion that, when a residential neighborhood changes its character and becomes a rooming-house area, slum, or foreign colony, the exist-

17

ing church may survive by becoming a mission, a settlement house, or a clubhouse. First Church has apparently retained much of its original character and design, despite the fact that the neighborhood has undergone change.

Kimball Young points out that:

Formerly the church was the focus of much neighborhood life. The Catholic churches have continued to be particularly effective as neighborhood centers because the membership is divided geographically into parishes in the same manner as voting precincts or school districts are laid out. This gives the particular pastor a chance to serve people who are themselves neighbors to each other and who already have attitudes of solidarity growing out of common life. The urban Protestant parish, for the most part, is not now divided on geographic lines, with the result that members are drawn from widespread areas. So long as the population remained fairly stationary, this handicap was overcome by the fact that the church buildings were located in the residential sections in which most of the members lived. Today in our rapidly growing American cities the situation is quite different. Many churches' edifices are left stranded in the midst of retail and wholesale districts or in cheap rooming houses or emerging slum areas just beyond the retail business section. The members are often so remote from the home church that they drift away to other parishes nearer or give up their church affiliation entirely.

In other ways the city church is caught in the changes of city life, especially in the growing emphasis upon secondary-group organization. Sophisticated urban populations are skeptical of what organized religion has to offer. There is frequently a conflict within the church body itself as to whether it shall liberalize its dogma, take up social service and educational and recreational programs, or stick by the old and the tried at the cost of younger membership and at the slow decay and final disappearance.[18]

Kimball Young is of the opinion that, when church edifices are stranded in the midst of retail and wholesale districts, or in cheap rooming-house or emerging slum areas, the members are often so remote from their home church that they drift away to other parishes nearer by or give up their church affiliation entirely.

Gist and Halbert note that:

Churches with a high ratio of young persons tend to grow rapidly and to have compact parishes, whereas those with a complex and varied program grow slowly, have a wide scattering of constituents, and are older in terms of chronological age. Older churches, which are "socially mature" institutions, tend to be located near the center of the city in areas characterized by various forms of social deterioration, but churches with a high ratio of young persons are apt to be in districts considerably removed from the central zones.[19] One would assume that First Church, with a history of one hundred and nine years in the Atlanta community, has reached social maturity and might maintain its place of location in the Atlanta community.

Landis observed in his study of movements that:

New adjustments are sometimes difficult to make; in fact, they may be so difficult in many cases that the individual shuns new associations and does not participate in community life as he normally would. Adults who move frequently often lose interest in church and quit going rather than face the adjustments involved in becoming acquainted with a new group.[20]

Landis feels that, in moving, people are faced with the problem of adjustment and fail to participate in a new community and the church because the adjustments are hard to make.

CHAPTER II

RESIDENTIAL PATTERNS OF THE MEMBERSHIP

This chapter seeks to describe and compare the residential distributions in the successive ten-year periods between 1910 and 1950. It should be remembered that our hypotheses are that significant shifts occur in the population, that the population of the latter years is more dispersed than the population of the earlier years, and that the residential areas of members of this old and high-status church are in keeping with their status.

Table 1 shows the number and percent of Atlanta membership by census tracts for the respective census periods.[1] The data show that the membership reported for these census periods ranged between a low of 215 for 1920 and a high of 497 for 1910. In 1910, 497 members were dispersed over 29 census tracts, with one-third of them in census tract F–28 immediately surrounding the church. In 1920, just after World War I, 215 were dispersed over 23 tracts, with one-fourth in tract F–28. In 1930, 453 members were scattered over 21 census tracts, with slightly more than one-third in tract F–28; in 1940, 351 members were scattered over 28 census tracts, with about one-eighth living in census tract

21

TABLE 1
DISTRIBUTION OF ATLANTA MEMBERSHIP OF FIRST CHURCH BY CENSUS TRACTS FOR 1910, 1920, 1930, 1940, AND 1950, BY NUMBER AND PERCENT

Census Tract Numbers	1910 Number	1910 Percent	1920 Number	1920 Percent	1930 Number	1930 Percent	1940 Number	1940 Percent	1950 Number	1950 Percent
F – 28	163	32.8	50	23.2	165	36.4	48	13.6	43	9.4
F – 29	88	17.7	47	21.8	78	17.2	66	18.9	36	7.8
F – 26	31	6.2	5	2.3	0	0	4	*	8	1.7
F – 18	27	5.4	12	5.6	28	4.6	20	5.7	24	6.2
F – 25	24	4.9	7	3.2	32	7.0	22	6.2	20	4.3
F – 43	16	3.2	2	*	0	0	2	*	7	1.5
F – 55	13	2.6	2	*	7	1.5	2	*	6	1.3
F – 35	11	2.2	3	*	0	0	1	*	2	*
F – 33	11	2.2	7	3.2	22	4.8	18	5.1	8	1.7
F – 27	11	2.2	5	2.5	8	1.8	2	*	2	*
F – 19	11	2.2	4	*	8	1.8	2	*	*	*
F – 38	7	1.4	1	*	24	5.3	60	17.0	43	9.3
F – 56	7	1.4	0	0	0	0	0	0	5	1.0
F – 22	6	1.2	0	0	1	*	0	0	5	1.0
D – 6	5	1.0	4	*	0	0	0	0	1	*
D – 8	4	*	1	*	5	1.1	1	*	2	*
F – 44	5	*	0	0	2	*	0	0	0	0
F – 21	3	*	2	*	8	1.8	0	0	0	0
F – 48	3	*	2	*	5	1.1	7	1.9	7	1.5
F – 62	2	*	0	0	0	0	0	0	0	0
DC – 24	1	*	0	0	0	0	24	6.8	88	19.2
DC – 4	1	*	0	0	0	0	0	0	0	0
F – 5	1	*	0	0	0	0	0	0	0	0
FC – 2	1	*	0	0	0	0	0	0	0	0
F – 39	1	*	0	0	0	0	37	10.5	28	6.1
F – 58	1	*	0	0	0	0	0	0	0	0
F – 12	1	*	1	*	0	0	0	0	0	0
F – 47	1	*	1	*	0	0	0	0	1	*

	#	%	#	%	#	%	#	%	#	%
F – 11	1	*	0	0	1	5.5	0	0	0	0
F – 36	0	0	13	6.0	25	*	9	2.5	5	1.0
F – 42	0	0	6	2.7	1	0	1	*	2	*
FC – 16	0	0	6	2.7	0	*	0	0	0	0
FC – 5	0	0	1	*	1	0	0	0	0	0
D – 2	0	0	1	*	0	1.3	0	*	1	*
FC – 7	0	0	0	0	6	*	4	1.4	13	2.8
F – 40	0	0	0	0	2	*	5	*	17	3.7
F – 17	0	0	0	0	1	0	1	1.4	7	1.5
F – 23	0	0	0	0	0	0	5	1.4	10	2.2
F – 37	0	0	0	0	0	0	5	*	9	2.0
F – 63	0	0	0	0	0	0	3	*	8	1.7
F – 16	0	0	0	0	0	0	4	*	5	1.0
F – 57	0	0	0	0	0	0	3	*	3	*
FC – 15	0	0	0	0	0	0	1	*	0	0
F – 46	0	0	0	0	0	0	1	0	4	*
F – 7	0	0	0	0	0	0	0	0	1	*
F – 8	0	0	0	0	0	0	0	0	2	*
FC – 20	0	0	0	0	0	0	0	0	3	*
D – 9	0	0	0	0	0	0	0	0	4	*
FC – 11	0	0	0	0	0	0	0	0	2	*
FC – 9	0	0	0	0	0	0	0	0	3	*
Out-of-town	19		7		8		3		10	
No address	20		25		9				7	
No census tract	16				13					
Total	427		215		453		351		458	

TABLE 2
THE NUMBER OF MEMBERS OF FIRST CHURCH
ENROLLED FOR 1910, 1920, 1930, 1940, AND 1950

Years	Number of Members
1910	497
1920	215
1930	453
1940	351
1950	458

TABLE 3
THE NUMBER OF TRACTS IN WHICH
MEMBERS OF FIRST CHURCH
RESIDED IN 1910, 1920, 1930, 1940, AND 1950

Years	Number of Tracts
1910	29
1920	23
1930	21
1940	28
1950	37

F–28; in 1950, there were 458 living in 37 census tracts. The greatest dispersion of population occurred after 1930 and coincided with the expansion of the downtown business district of Atlanta and the expansion of the Negro community on the west side of Atlanta.

In the following sections, a more detailed analysis of the distribution of the Atlanta members for the respective periods will be made.

THE RESIDENTIAL PATTERN OF 1910

In an interview with an old member of 1910, we get the comment:

In 1910 we had on the sidewalk in front of First Church a pump that supplied water for horses and people. People came in their buggies to church and the other activities and stayed. The community meant everything.

In 1910, First Church had a listed membership of 497. One-half (50.5 percent) of the membership of this period lived in what are now census tracts F–28 and F–29, which embrace the immediate vicinity of the church. At that time, 32.8 percent were in tract F–28[2] and 17.7 percent in tract F–29.[3] Table 4 shows the 1910 distribution of members by census tracts. The other one-half (49.5 percent) of the members were scattered throughout twenty-seven other census tracts. Table 4 reveals that 6.2 percent were living in what is now tract F–36.[4] This area is on the west side of town and is approximately one and one-half miles from the church. In 1910, according to an old resident, "one found some of your better families living on Tatnall, Walnut, and Fair Streets." This area is close to the "Old Atlanta University"—now Morris Brown College. In this neighborhood now are the E. A. Ware School, named

25

TABLE 4
NUMBER AND PERCENT OF MEMBERSHIP
OF FIRST CHURCH
BY CENSUS TRACTS FOR 1910

Census Tract Numbers	Number	Percent
F – 28	163	32.8
F – 29	88	17.7
F – 36	31	6.2
F – 18	27	5.4
F – 26	24	4.9
F – 43	16	3.2
F – 55	13	2.6
F – 35	11	2.2
F – 33	11	2.2
F – 27	11	2.2
F – 19	11	2.2
F – 38	7	1.4
F – 56	7	1.4
F – 22	6	1.2
D – 6	5	1.0
D – 8	4	*
F – 44	5	*
F – 21	3	*
F – 48	3	*
F – 62	2	*
F – 24	1	*
DC – 4	1	*
F – 5	1	*
FC – 2	1	*
F – 39	1	*
F – 58	1	*
F – 12	1	*
F – 47		*
F – 11	1	*
Total	455	100.0

*Less than one percent

FIGURE 1

THE RESIDENTIAL PATTERN OF DISTRIBUTION OF MEMBERS OF
FIRST CHURCH FOR 1910

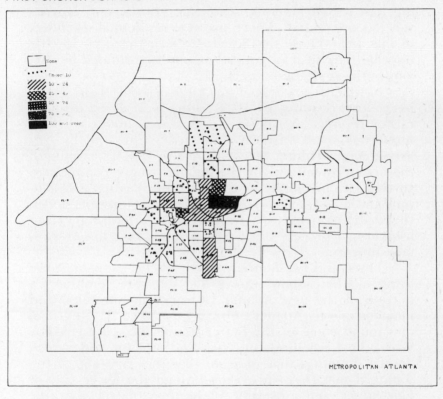

for the first president of Atlanta University; Friendship Baptist Church, located on Mitchell Street and one of the historic markers in the Atlanta community; and the West Mitchell Methodist Church.

Five and four-tenths percent of the 1910 membership resided in what is now tract F–18.[5] This area is close to the church and is one that has undergone marked change. It is now an area where garages, parking lots, service stations, wholesale houses, and moving van lots are found. There are few residential dwellings in this area. Those that are located in this area for the most part are in poor condition, and surrounded by various business establishments.

In what is now tract F–25,[6] 4.9 percent of the members were residing in 1910. This is a west-side area rather recently expanded. In this area today, we find numerous small business enterprises operated by Negroes. Along Hunter Street to Ashby, one finds some of the better restaurants of the Atlanta Negro community. In this area are located Frazier's Cafe, Paschal's Restaurant and many smaller eating places, two ten-cent stores, three drugstores, two or three dry-cleaning establishments, a grocery store, and several other business establishments.

Three and two-tenths percent of the members were living in what is now tract F–43.[7] This area embraces a portion of the new Atlanta University community, and includes one of Atlanta's housing projects. At one time, one found some of the better homes located on Ashby Street. One will find on West-End Avenue today residential dwellings that indicate that they are not of the standard that they once were. Along the lower end of Fair Street, and especially in the area that at one time was called "The Bottom," we find a small-business district, including two or three grocery stores, a drugstore, a ten-cent store, a dairy, a service station, a shoe shop, a beauty parlor, and two or three other business establishments.

Two and six-tenths percent of the members were living in tract F–55.[8] A portion of this area embraces what at one time was Clark College, today Carver Vocational School. There is also located in this south Atlanta community on McDonough Boulevard, Gammon Theological Seminary. One will also find on McDonough Boulevard a theater, two or three grocery stores, a barbershop, and a few other business establishments that serve the community. For the most part, the houses that are in this area, especially along Capitol Avenue, Atlanta Avenue, and Georgia Avenue, are the old two-story type of dwelling.

Two and two-tenths percent of the members lived in tract F–33.[9] This section is near the church. One will find on Butler the Young Men's Christian Association, Bronner Brothers' Beauty Supply company, a funeral parlor, and dilapidated residential dwellings. Along Edgewood Avenue, one will find any number of business establishments that serve the community.

Two and two-tenths percent of the members were also found living in tract F–27.[10] We find this section not too far removed from the church. This area now embraces a number of dilapidated houses that are rapidly being closed in upon by the business expansion that is taking place in this community. This section merges with the business, wholesale, and manufacturing areas.

Two and two-tenths percent of the members lived in tract F–19.[11] Tract F–19 also is now an area where one will find any number of business establishments and few residences.

One and four-tenths percent of the members were in tract F–56.[12] Tract F–56 is an area that for the most part includes residential dwellings.

One and two-tenths percent of the members were found living in tract F–22.[13] Tract F–22 is a section of residences and businesses.

One percent had residence in tract D–6.[14] Tract D–6 is in Decatur.

THE RESIDENTIAL PATTERN OF 1920

The records of First Church show a fifty-seven per-cent decline in the membership for 1920 over that for 1910. For 1920, the total enrolled was 215, as against 497 in 1910. This decline might be explained by the conditions immediately following World War I and the heavy mi-gration of Negroes to the North and East. Informants mention these as factors responsible for the decline in the membership of First Church at this time. In 1920, as in 1910, we find that the majority of the members lived in what are now census tracts F–28 and F–29.[15] Twenty-three and two-tenths percent of the members were found living in tract F–29. In 1920, this area had not been exposed to the expansion of the business sections of Atlanta as it has since. It was at that time, according to an older member of the community, a rather stable community.

Table 5 reveals the number and percent of mem-bers by census tracts for 1920. Table 5 shows that 2.3 percent of the members lived in tract F–26.[16] This is a west-side community. Today, Davis, Mitchell, and Vine Streets are notorious centers characterized by a high ratio of disorganization. Houses in this area are in poor con-dition. This community is about one and one-fourths miles from First Church.

Five and six-tenths percent of the members were in tract F–18 in 1920; three and two-tenths percent in tract F–25; three and two-tenths percent in tract F–33; two and three-tenths percent in tract F–27 and six percent in tract F–36.[17]

Two and seven-tenths percent of the members were in tract F–42.[18] This is a west-side community. During this early period, the majority of the members living in tract F–42 were near or on Ashby Street and West-End Avenue. In recent years, the Negro has moved into the Gordon Road area. This section is about two and one-

TABLE 5
NUMBER AND PERCENT OF MEMBERSHIP OF FIRST CHURCH BY CENSUS TRACTS FOR 1920

Census Tract Numbers	Number	Percent
F – 28	50	23.2
F – 29	47	21.8
F – 26	5	2.3
F – 18	12	5.6
F – 25	7	3.2
F – 43	2	*
F – 55	2	*
F – 35	3	*
F – 33	7	3.2
F – 27	5	2.3
F – 19	4	*
F – 38	1	*
F – 56	0	*
F – 22	0	*
D – 6	4	*
D – 8	1	*
F – 44	0	*
F – 21	2	*
F – 48	2	*
F – 12	1	*
F – 47	1	*
F – 36	13	6.0
F – 42	6	2.7
FC – 16	6	2.7
FC – 5	1	*
D – 2	1	*
Total	183	100.0

*Less than one percent

FIGURE 2

THE RESIDENTIAL PATTERN OF DISTRIBUTION OF MEMBERS OF
FIRST CHURCH FOR 1920

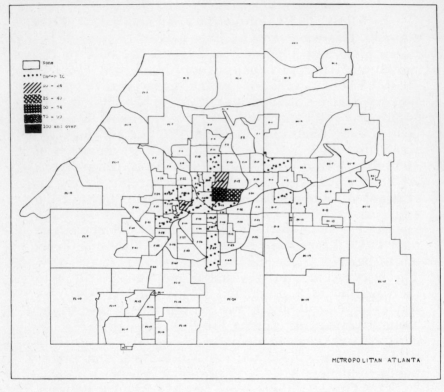

half miles or more from First Church. Two and seven-tenths percent of the members are in tract FC–16, which is a Fulton County community.

Figure 2 gives a graphic presentation of the distribution of the membership of the church for 1920.

THE RESIDENTIAL PATTERN OF 1930

In 1930, 453 members were enrolled at First Church. This represents an increase of 110 percent between 1920 and 1930. We still found the bulk of the members living in census tracts F–28 and F–29 in 1930.[19] The data indicate that 53.6 percent of the members lived in the immediate vicinity of the church, that is, in tracts F–28 and F–29. In 1910, we found 50.5 percent in these tracts, and in 1920, 45.0 percent. Figure 3 shows that there is a wider distribution of members in 1930 than in the preceding periods. More census tracts are represented, with some of the more remote areas increasing in numbers. Four and six-tenths percent of the members were found living in tract F–18; seven percent in tract F–25; 1.5 percent in tract F–55; 4.8 percent in tract F–33; 1.8 percent in tract F–19.[20] Five and three-tenths percent of the membership lived in tract F–38.[21] This tract includes an area that at one time, according to the daughter of a prominent Negro minister who now resides on Tatnall Street, was an area where some of the "better" families of Atlanta lived. Along Fair Street today, one will find a comparatively new Negro church, a housing project, a theater, a business area, and single-family residences.

On Tatnall Street, one finds a beauty college, Cooper's Soda and Lunch Place, Ted Lewis Dry Cleaners, a Baptist church, a store, a beauty parlor, Lucas Grill, a number of residences that are in need of repair, and the new Phyllis Wheatley Branch of the Y.W.C.A.

TABLE 6
NUMBER AND PERCENT OF MEMBERSHIP
OF FIRST CHURCH
BY CENSUS TRACTS FOR 1930

Census Tract Numbers	Number	Percent
F – 28	165	36.4
F – 29	78	17.2
F – 18	28	4.6
F – 25	32	7.0
F – 55	7	1.5
F – 35	22	4.8
F – 27	8	1.8
F – 19	8	1.8
F – 38	24	5.3
F – 32	1	*
D – 8	5	1.1
F – 44	2	*
F – 21	8	1.8
F – 48	5	1.1
F – 11	1	*
F – 36	25	5.5
FC – 7	6	1.3
F – 40	2	*
F – 17	1	*
Total	426	100.0

FIGURE 3

THE RESIDENTIAL PATTERN OF DISTRIBUTION OF MEMBERS OF FIRST CHURCH FOR 1930

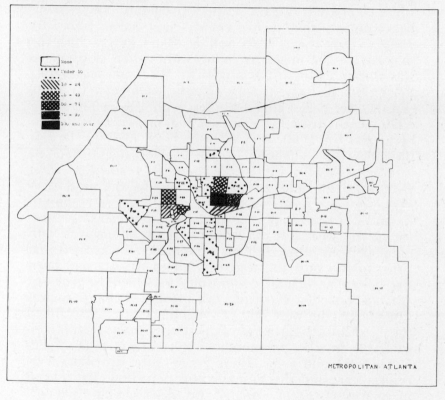

METROPOLITAN ATLANTA

Elm, Walnut, Parson, Maner, and Lawshe Streets are mostly residential sections.

THE RESIDENTIAL PATTERN OF 1940

In 1940, First Church carried on its rolls 351 members. This number represents a 22.5 percent decrease when compared with the 1930 entrollment. These members were distributed over twenty-eight census tracts. By 1940, census tracts F–28 and F–29 no longer had the majority of the members living within their borders, as was true in 1910, 1920, and 1930. We find census tract F–29 ranking highest, with sixty-six members. In 1910, census tract F–28 ranked highest with 163 members. In 1920, census tract F–28 ranked highest with fifty members, and, in 1930, census tract F–28 had the largest number—165 members. In 1910, seven members lived in tract F–38; in 1920, one member resided in tract F–38; and in 1930, twenty-four members found residence in tract F–38. Tract F–38 is a west-side community and it was around 1940 that we found growing interest in the west side of Atlanta. From interviews with older persons of the Atlanta community, we learned that prior to this time the fourth ward of Atlanta had been the better residential community to which Negroes of Atlanta looked with pride, but around 1940 there was the shift to the west side of Atlanta. Tract F–28 ranked third, with forty-eight members. Other tracts with a considerable number of members were tracts F–18, F–22, F–33, F–24, and F–39. Table 7 shows the distribution by census tract and the number and percentage who lived in each tract. From Table 7, we observe that 13.6 percent of the members were found living in tract F–28; 18.9 percent in tract F–29; 5.7 percent in tract F–18; 6.2 percent in tract F–25; 5.1 percent in F–33; 17.0 percent in F–38; 1.9 percent in F–48, and 2.5 percent in F–36.[22]

TABLE 7
NUMBER AND PERCENT OF MEMBERSHIP
OF FIRST CHURCH
BY CENSUS TRACTS FOR 1940

Census Tract Numbers	Number	Percent
F – 28	48	13.6
F – 29	66	18.9
F – 26	4	*
F – 18	20	5.7
F – 25	22	6.2
F – 43	2	*
F – 55	2	*
F – 35	1	*
F – 33	18	5.1
F – 27	2	*
F – 19	2	*
F – 38	60	17.0
D – 8	1	*
F – 48	7	1.9
F – 24	24	6.8
F – 39	37	10.5
F – 36	9	2.5
F – 42	1	*
FC – 7	4	*
F – 40	5	1.4
F – 17	1	*
F – 23	5	1.4
F – 37	5	1.4
F – 63	3	*
F – 16	4	*
F – 57	3	*
FC – 15	1	*
F – 46	1	*
Total	327	100.0

*Less than one percent

37

FIGURE 4

THE RESIDENTIAL PATTERN OF DISTRIBUTION OF MEMBERS OF
FIRST CHURCH FOR 1940

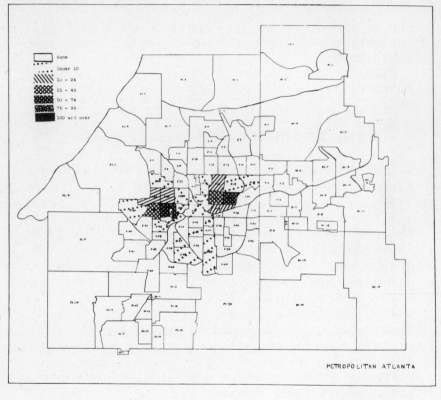

In tract F–24, there was 6.8 percent.[23] In this area, we found some of the better Negro homes of the Atlanta community.[24] Ten and five-tenths percent of the members were found living in tract F–39.[25] Tract F–39 includes the Mozley Drive area, which is a new area for Negroes. It had formerly been occupied by whites. One and four-tenths percent of the members lived in tract F–40.[26] Tract F–40 also includes a portion of the Mozley Drive community, which had also recently become available as a residential section for Negroes. In tract F–23,[27] we find one and four-tenths percent of the members of First Church.

Figure 4 reveals the decreasing concentration of members in the immediate vicinity of the church.

THE RESIDENTIAL PATTERN OF 1950

In 1950, there were 458 members enrolled at First Church, representing a thirty percent increase over 1940.

The residential pattern of 1950 presents a picture altogether different from the one shown in 1910, 1920, 1930, and 1940. By 1950, the largest percentage of the members were found living in tract F–34[28]—a west-side community. We find the members scattered over more census tracts than at any other period. In 1910, they resided in twenty-nine different tracts. In 1920, they were distributed throughout twenty-six different census tracts. In 1930, they found residence in twenty census tracts; 1940 found them spread out in twenty-eight different tracts; and 1950's residential pattern showed them living in thirty-seven tracts. With an increase in the number of tracts in which the members enrolled at First Church resided in 1950, dispersion rather than concentration characterizes the membership. Table 8 shows the number and percent of the membership by census tract in 1950.

TABLE 8
NUMBER AND PERCENT OF MEMBERSHIP
OF FIRST CHURCH
BY CENSUS TRACTS FOR 1950

Census Tract Numbers	Number	Percent
F – 28	43	9.4
F – 29	36	7.8
F – 26	8	1.7
F – 18	24	5.2
F – 25	20	4.3
F – 43	7	1.5
F – 55	6	1.3
F – 35	2	*
F – 33	8	1.7
F – 27	2	*
F – 38	43	9.3
F – 56	5	1.0
F – 22	5	1.0
D – 6	1	*
D – 8	2	*
F – 48	7	1.5
F – 24	88	19.2
F – 39	28	6.1
F – 47	1	*
F – 36	5	1.0
F – 42	2	*
D – 2	1	*
FC – 7	13	2.8
F – 40	17	3.7
F – 17	7	1.5
F – 23	10	2.2
F – 37	9	2.0
F – 63	8	1.7
F – 16	5	1.0
F – 57	3	*
F – 46	4	*
F – 7	1	*
F – 8	2	*
FC – 20	3	*
D – 9	4	*
FC – 11	2	*
FC – 9	3	*
Total	435	100.0

*Less than one percent

FIGURE 5

THE RESIDENTIAL PATTERN OF DISTRIBUTION OF MEMBERS OF
FIRST CHURCH FOR 1950

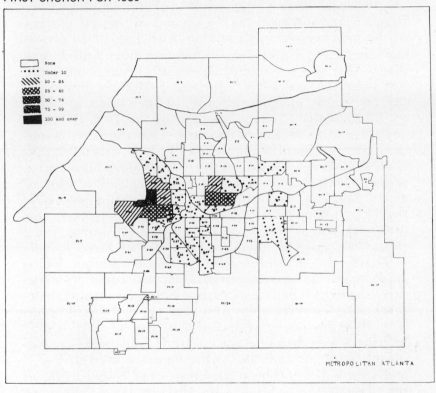

In tract F–29, 9.4 percent of the membership was found; 7.8 percent in tract F–29; 5.2 percent in tract F–18, 4.3 percent in F–25; 1.3 percent in F–55; 1.7 percent in F–33; 9.3 percent in F–38; 19.2 percent in F–24; 6.1 percent in F–39; 1.0 percent in F–36; 2.8 percent in FC–7; 3.7 percent in F–40; 1.5 percent in F–43; 1.0 percent in F–56; 1.0 percent in F–22; 1.5 percent in F–48; and 2.2 percent in F–23.[29]

One and seven-tenths percent of the members were found living in tract F–26.[30] One and five-tenths percent of the membership was found in tract F–17.[31] In census tract F–37,[32] 2.0 percent of the members found residence. One and seven-tenths percent of the membership was found in tract F–63.[33] In tract F–16,[34] we found 1.0 percent of the members residing. Other tracts in which we find less than five members living are D–2, D–8, and D–9. These areas are in Decatur. Less than five members are also found living in tract F–35.[35] Tract F–35 includes the lower portion of the Fair-Walker Street area, which has undergone a number of changes as a result of a new highway. According to the area rating set-up by the Department of Sociology of Atlanta University, this area would rate "poor." Two members are found living in tract F–27.[36] One member lived in tract F–47.[37] Tract F–47 includes the Summerhill section of Atlanta, which ranks "poor" as a residential area, according to structures needing repair, structures without basement, structures unfit for occupancy, and overcrowded dwelling units.[38] Two members were found living in tract F–42[39] and three were living in tract F–57.[40] Four members had found residence in F–46.[41] One member lived in F–7,[42] and two in F–8.[43] Three members were found living in tract FC–20, two in FC–11, and three in FC–9. These are Fulton County areas for which we have no description. Figure 5 shows the distribution of members in the various census tracts.

CHAPTER III

RESIDENTIAL MOBILITY AMONG THE MEMBERSHIP

This chapter is designed to describe the movements of members of First Church by ten-year periods—1920, 1930, 1940, and 1950. With the use of a scaled map of the city of Atlanta and a ruler, the writer was able to measure the distance of the movements of the members who were selected in a manner described in chapter I. Addresses were compared for two successive ten-year periods. Those who were members in 1910 were compared with those that were members in 1920; those of 1920 with those of 1930; those of 1930 with those of 1940; and those of 1940 with those of 1950.

Of the one hundred forty-eight names that appeared in both 1910 and 1920 registers, eighteen, or 12.1 percent, had moved. That is, the 1910 register showed a change of address of eighteen persons whose names had also appeared in the 1920 register but at a different address.

When we check in a similar manner the members whose names appear in the 1920 and 1930 registers, we notice that fifteen, or 10.9 percent, of the one hundred thirty-seven members who appeared in both registers had moved.

TABLE 9
DISTANCES MOVED BY SELECTED MEMBERS OF FIRST CHURCH
FOR 1920, 1930, 1940, AND 1950

Miles	1920		1930		1940		1950	
	Frequency	Cumulative Frequency	Frequency	Cumulative Frequency	Frequency	Cumulative Frequency	Frequency	Cumulative Frequency
0 – .5	-	-	1	1	6	6	3	3
.5 – .9	3	3	6	7	7	13	11	14
1.0 – 1.4	3	6	1	8	3	16	7	21
1.5 – 1.9	2	8	2	10	5	21	4	25
2.0 – 2.4	2	10	2	12	3	24	6	31
2.5 – 2.9	-	-	2	14	1	25	1	32
3.0 – 3.4	3	13	1	-	4	29	-	-
3.5 – 3.9	-	-	-	-	-	-	-	-
4.0 – 4.4	1	14	-	-	-	-	2	34
4.5 – 4.9	-	-	-	-	-	-	-	-
5.0 – 5.4	-	-	-	-	2	31	1	35
5.5 – 5.9	-	-	-	-	-	-	-	-
Total	14		15		31		35	

44

In comparing the members who appeared in both the 1930 and 1940 registers, there were thirty-one, or 26.6 percent, who had moved from their 1930 addresses. When checking the 1940 and 1950 registers for names that appear at both periods, we noticed an increase in the number of movements. Thirty-eight, or 16.7 percent, of the one hundred sixty-seven names that appeared at both periods moved.

In the sections that follow, there is a more detailed description of the movements and distance of the movements for each period under study.

THE PATTERN OF MOVEMENT OF 1920

The membership figures are markedly smaller for 1920 as indicated in the discussion of distribution of residence for 1920. The total membership as of this date is 215.

In examining the membership rolls for 1910 and 1920, we find that there are one hundred forty-eight persons whose names appeared at both periods. Of these one hundred forty-eight names that appeared at both periods, eighteen had moved to a different address.

When we compare the 1910 and 1920 rolls, we find a decrease in the membership. When we examine the records of those who were members in 1910 and in 1920, we find eighteen who have moved.

Let us examine the type of movement that is represented in the mobile people, which ranged from 0.8 to 4.4 miles.

Table 10 reveals that three members moved from 0.5 to 0.9 miles; three from 1.0 to 1.4 miles; two from 1.5 to 1.9 miles; two from 2.0 to 2.4 miles; three from 3.0 to 3.4 miles; and one from 4.0 to 4.4 miles. The address of four of these mobile persons is unknown. The median distance for this period is about 1.5 miles. For

1930 is from 0.5 mile to 3.4 miles, wherein the range in 1920 was from 0.5 to 4.4 miles. No movement in 1930 was over 3.4 miles.

The median distance moved for this period is about 1.5 miles.

THE PATTERN OF MOVEMENT OF 1940

In 1940, First Church had a membership of 351 persons living in 28 census tracts. At this time, we find a decrease in the proportions living in the immediate vicinity of the church. The members were spread out more than at any preceding period. Around 1940, there seems to have been growing residential and commercial interest in the west side of Atlanta. According to old residents of the Atlanta community, the fourth ward in

TABLE 12
FREQUENCY DISTRIBUTION OF THE MOVEMENTS OF THIRTY-ONE MEMBERS OF FIRST CHURCH FOR 1940

Miles	Frequency	Cumulative Frequency
0 – .5	6	6
.5 – .9	7	13
1.0 – 1.4	3	16
1.5 – 1.9	5	21
2.0 – 2.4	3	24
2.5 – 2.9	1	25
3.0 – 3.4	4	29
3.5 – 3.9	-	-
4.0 – 4.4	-	
4.5 – 4.9	-	-
5.0 – 5.4	2	31
5.5 – 5.9	-	-
Total	31	

48

northeast Atlanta had been the community to which the Negroes looked with pride. Houston Street, Angier Avenue, and Pine Street and Boulevard had been the better residential areas in the Atlanta community. Around 1940, there started the westward movement. As we look at the 1940 movements, we are aware of the changing interest in the Negro community, and notice that the range in the movement during this period is from 0.5 to 5.4 miles. When compared with the preceding periods under study, we notice that the range for 1940 is greater than for 1920 and 1930. In 1920, the range was from 0.5 to 4.4 miles, and in 1930 the range was from 0.5 to 3.4 miles.

When we compare the membership rolls for 1930 and 1940, we find 115 persons whose names appear at both periods. Of the 115 names that appeared at both periods, 31 had moved to a different address. This is a number greater than in 1920 and 1930. In 1920, fifteen persons had moved, and in 1930, eighteen persons.

Table 12 shows the number and distance of these thirty-one movements. Six persons moved a distance less than 0.5 miles; seven moved from 0.5 to 0.9 miles; three moved from 1.0 to 1.4 miles; five from 1.5 to 1.9 miles; three from 2.0 to 2.4 miles; from 2.5 to 2.9 miles; four from 3.0 to 3.4 miles; and two from 5.0 to 5.4 miles. We notice that the movements during 1940 are more numerous than at any preceding period.

These mobile members have been found moving from Auburn to Ashby; from Leach to Ashby; from Vine to Randolph; from Greensferry to Newcastle; from Houston to Irwin; from Howell to University Place; from Baker to Ashby; from Haygood to Greensferry; from Johnson Avenue to Fair; from Howell to Boulevard; from Clark to Chestnut; and from Hilliard to Mitchell.

The median distance of the movement at this period is about 1.5 miles.

THE PATTERN OF MOVEMENT OF 1950

The pattern and rate of movement between 1940 and 1950 varied greatly from those presented in 1910, 1920, 1930 and 1940. Instead of finding the largest number in census tracts F–28 and F–29 as we have found in other periods, we find the largest number residing in census tract F–24, which is a west-side community where we have eighty-eight—or one in every five members—living. In 1910, we had one member living in census tract F–24; in 1920, none; in 1930, none; in 1940, twenty-four or 6.8 percent; and in 1950, eighty-eight or 19.2 percent.

In 1910, we found eighty-eight, or 17.7 percent, of the members, in tract F–28. In 1920, 50, or 23.2 percent; 1930, 165, or 36.4 percent; in 1940, 48, or 13.6 percent; and in 1950, 43, or 9.4 percent. The 1950 membership in census tract F–28 is a decline over the number in the preceding periods.

In 1910, we found eighty-eight, or 17.7 percent, of the members in census tract F–29. In 1920, forty-seven, or 21.8 percent; in 1930, seventy-eight, or 17.2 percent; in 1940, sixty-six, or 18.9 percent; and in 1950, thirty-six, or 7.8 percent. In census tract F–29, as in F–28, we notice a decline in the number of members in the 1950 pattern.

A greater number of movements are found taking place in 1950 than at any preceding period. In 1920, we found eighteen members moving from their 1910 place of address. In 1930, records showed that fifteen persons had moved from their 1920 place of residence. In 1940, thirty-one members had addresses that differed from the address that they had in 1930. In comparing the 1940 register with the 1950 register, we find 167 names listed in both registers. Of this 167 persons, thirty-eight have moved to a different address. This is an increase of seven over the 1940 movements. The 1950 movements

TABLE 13
FREQUENCY DISTRIBUTION OF THE MOVEMENTS OF THIRTY-EIGHT MEMBERS OF FIRST CHURCH FOR 1950

Miles	Frequency	Cumulative Frequency
0 – .5	3	3
.5 – .9	11	14
1.0 – 1.4	7	21
1.5 – 1.9	4	25
2.0 – 2.4	6	31
2.5 – 2.9	1	32
3.0 – 3.4	-	-
3.5 – 3.9	-	-
4.0 – 4.4	2	34
4.5 – 4.9	-	-
5.0 – 5.4	1	35
5.5 – 5.9	-	-
Total	35	

TABLE 14
DISTRIBUTION BY RATING OF RESIDENTIAL AREA OF 446 MEMBERS OF FIRST CHURCH, 1950

Rating of Areas	Number in Area	Percent
1	113	25.3
2	47	10.5
3	29	6.5
4	75	16.8
5	82	1.8
6	63	.1
7	37	2.9
Total	446	100.0

have not all been great distances. In a number of instances, they have been short.

Table 13 gives the number and distance of each of the movements in 1950. From Table 13, we are able to observe that three of the members moved a distance less than 0.5 miles; eleven moved a distance of 0.5 to 0.9 miles; seven moved from 1.0 to 1.4 miles; four moved 1.5 to 1.9 miles; six moved from 1.0 to 1.4 miles; six moved from 8.0 to 2.4 miles; one moved from 2.5 to 2.9 miles; two moved from 4.0 to 4.4 miles; and one from 5.0 to 5.4 miles. The median distance of the movements for this period is about 1.5 miles.

In 1950, we found members moving from Ashby to West-End Avenue; from Greensferry to Chicamauga; from Irwin to Hunter Road; from Fair to Hunter Road; from C Street to Hunter Road; from Houston to Booker Street; from Simpson Road to Mozley Drive; from Greensferry to Booker Street; from Larkin Street to Burbank; from Howell to Larkin Street; from Ashby Street to Sunset; from Howell to Leathers Circle; from Greensferry to Chapel Road; and from Palmetto Avenue to Beckwith.

An area rating prepared by the Department of Sociology of Atlanta University gives insight into the characteristics of the various residential communities in which we find the members of First Church residing. Members of First Church have residence in these various areas to which there has been attached a value. The rating has the following values: 1, very high; 2, high; 3, above average; 4, average; 5, below average; 6, low; and 7, very low. Table 14 shows the number of members finding residence in the various areas.

Twenty-six listed persons have no address given; ten live out-of-town. We were unable to locate the area six lived in.

From Table 14, we observe that, in 1950, one-fourth of the members are found living in an area with a rating of one. More members live in an area of this highest classification than in any other. The second largest number is found in an area with a rating of five; the third largest in an area with a rating of four; and the fourth largest in an area with a rating of six. Ten and five-tenths percent live in an area with a rating of two, which is high. Two and nine-tenths percent of the members are found in an area with a rating of seven, which is very low. Fewer members are found in an area with a rating of three, which is above average.

In tracing the movements from 1910 to 1950, we notice that three families have been found living at the same address in 1910, 1920, 1930, 1940, and 1950. Family number one lives in the fourth ward, formerly a status community in Atlanta. Family number two lives on the west side in the vicinity of the old Atlanta University. Family number three lives in south Atlanta, in the vicinity of Gammon Theological Seminary. One family has moved a short distance in this forty-year period. This movement has been on the same street.

Not only has there been a general movement on the part of the members of First Church, but the church parsonage has also been a part of this movement. It was at one time in the immediate vicinity of the church. It later moved to Angier Avenue, which was the community in which the members lived. It is now located on the west side of town.

THE OUT-OF-TOWN MOVEMENTS

For each period under study, we noticed that there have been some movements that have been out-of-town. In checking the 1920 register, we find eight members living at out-of-town addresses. The out-of-town distribution is as follows: Camp McClellan, three; Fisk University, Nashville, Tennessee, one; Decatur, Georgia, one; Des Moines, Iowa, one; Greenville, South Carolina, one; and McDonough, Georgia, one.

In 1930, we find an out-of-town distribution of members. One member has moved from Randolph Street to Evanston, Illinois, and another member from Greensferry Street to Des Moines, Iowa. Other out-of-town members are distributed as follows: Buffalo, New York, one; Cotton Valley, Georgia, one; Oakland, California, one; Memphis, Tennessee, one; Decatur, Georgia, one; and Columbia, South Carolina, one.

We find only two out-of-town movements in 1940. One member moved from Linden Street to Detroit, Michigan, and another from Auburn Avenue to Baltimore, Maryland.

As we trace the out-of-town movements for 1950, we find that one member has moved from Bedford Place to Washington, D.C., and another from Bedford Place to the United States Army. One person moved from Parson Street to Africa; one from Piedmont to Montgomery, Alabama, and two from Randolph Street to Tuskegee, Alabama. The following are also found at out-of-town addresses: one, Monticello, Georgia; one, Birmingham, Alabama; one, Waynesboro, Georgia, and one, Decatur, Georgia.

CHAPTER IV

SUMMARY AND CONCLUSIONS

This study of the membership of First Church, a high-status church in the Atlanta community, has focused on the residential distribution and mobility of the membership over the period 1910–1950. This has been accomplished by using five ten-year interval samplings of the membership roll.

An important characteristic of this church is that it is a high-status church that is apparently marooned in a low-status neighborhood; it draws a large proportion of its members from more distant and higher status communities.

The data show that the church has had an important influence in the Atlanta community. From the beginning, it has been a central place in the Negro community for educational, fraternal, civic, and community gatherings.

In studying the membership of this church, we have sought to describe (1) the changes in the spatial distribution of the members; (2) the types of residential movement; and (3) the extent of the movements over a forty-year period.

The basic assumption underlying the study was that the spatial redistribution of the members of this church reflects the growth and expansion of the Negro community, with its consequent increase in occupational differentiation and pressure for new and better location. Among the hypotheses guiding the collection of data were these: (1) the percentage of members living in the immediate vicinity of First Church has consistently declined, in keeping with the changing social and economic characteristics of the area; (2) current membership of First Church is dispersed over a significantly wider area than the earlier membership; and (3) a significant proportion of the membership of First Church lives in residential districts that are rated high by objective indices and community consensus. The data give positive support for all of these propositions. Specific findings and some of their implications may now be summarized.

Over a period of fifty years, the residential center of the membership of First Church has shifted from an area within a few blocks of the church westwardly. This westward movement of the church population has coincided with changes in the Atlanta community and within the Negro subcommunity. As the central business district has expanded, residential areas near the church have been blighted. As occupational differentiation and economic advance have progressed in the Negro community, there has occurred significant expansion and mobility. It appears that many of the leaders in this differentiation and community expansion have been members of First Church and their associates. Our tables and charts show that a rapid residential dispersion began around 1940, and has continued over the last ten or twelve years. One result of this movement has been that a significantly large proportion of the membership now resides in the relatively new west-side communities, which are ranked among those most desirable for Negro occupancy.

Concrete indications of the dispersion are seen in the fact that the two census tracts in the immediate vicinity of the church contained more than fifty percent of the membership in 1910, 1920, and 1930. Today, less than one in five of the members live in these two tracts; and the tract with the greatest concentration of members is now tract F–24, in which approximately twenty percent of the members live. In 1910, members were dispersed over twenty-nine tracts. In 1950, they were dispersed over thirty-seven tracts.

Another indication of the characteristics of the residential communities in which we find the members of First Church residing is obtained when residences are classified by the rating of residential areas. Using an area rating prepared by the Department of Sociology of Atlanta University, we found that over twenty-five percent of the members lived in areas with a rating of one, very high; and over ten percent lived in areas with a rating of two, high. This finding takes on added significance when it is compared with the findings with respect to the membership of another Atlanta church, the Ebenezer Baptist Church. Edward Arthur Balridge, in a study, "Some Factors Related to Membership and Participation in an Urban Protestant Church,"[1] found only six percent of the Ebenezer Baptist Church's 1950 membership lived in areas rated one; and one percent lived in areas rated two. Nearly two out of three members of this church (Ebenezer) lived in areas rated six and seven, low and very low.

In an effort to obtain some measure of the rate of movement, addresses were compared for successive ten-year periods. Those who were members in 1910 were compared with those who were members in 1920; those in 1920 with those of 1930; those of 1930 with those of 1940; and those of 1940 with those of 1950. In these respective periods, names and addresses were checked in order to list those who had moved. The data indicate that the movements in the earlier periods were relatively fewer and shorter. However, the data with respect to distance moved do not show the striking differences between earlier and late periods that residential distribution figures show.

Our findings provide the picture of an old, prestige-laden church—with a large proportion of its members differentiated socially and economically from the mass of the Negro population—which is stranded. The continuation of the church at its present physical location is probably a reflection in part of sentiment and inertia, and the fact that distance is not too important a deterrent because of the automobile. There is increasing awareness on the part of the officers and members of the church of the disparity between ecological site and location and the residence and social status of members. It appears inevitable that this church will move; there are few indications of plans to change functions and characteristics to conform to the needs and characteristics of the immediate area and its population.

Our findings are in general agreement with the already-cited findings of students of the church and urban institutions such as H. Paul Douglass, Wilson and Kolb, Hughes, and Gist and Halbert.

The comparison of our findings with respect to First Church, an old and high-status church, with the findings of Balridge with respect to Ebenezer Baptist Church is suggestive that further studies of the characteristics of members of Negro urban churches are needed to spell out more clearly differences in types and differences in patterns of membership participation and support—plus more indication of the historical, cultural, ecological, and social-psychological factors operative.

CHAPTER V

EPILOGUE

The black church in the Atlanta community has been and continues to be a potent force in the community.

In the case of First Church, there were those who occupied a relatively high socioeconomic status in the community who were engaged in improving the quality of life for the black minority.

Martin Luther King, Jr., who grew up a few blocks from First Church, was a member of Ebenezer Baptist Church which had been pastored by his grandfather, an exponent of civil rights, and later by his father, had the support of the lower and lower-middle socioeconomic levels. The membership of Ebenezer lived in close proximity to the church until recent years. The membership represented a cross section of the black population.

Those persons comprising the lower and lower-middle classes for the most part were found in such occupations as cooks, maids, mechanics, and railroad workers, while there were others in such occupations as teachers, nurses, and other professions, but all found an opportunity to share in the church life at Ebenezer.

The black church has had a tremendous impact in the uprising of the blacks in the Atlanta community. This impact is twofold—one is relating to the church as a denominational institution, and another is the church as an institution for political awakening.

The African Methodist Episcopal church came into being as a protest. Richard Allen refused to be treated as less than a person, less than a first-class citizen, and, as a result of his protest against the Methodist church, walked out of Old St. George Church in Philadelphia and started the African Methodist Episcopal church. This spirit was reflected in Allen Temple A.M.E. Church during the more recent years of protest when it was pastored by John Albert Middleton, himself actively engaged in the marches that were led by Martin Luther King, Jr. Allen Temple could boast of having the first black city councilman—Q. V. Williamson—as one of her members. Williamson still holds this post. It was in Allen Temple that Operation Breadbasket was organized, which served as an organization to provide job opportunities in businesses that had discriminated against blacks and to upgrade blacks in businesses that had previously kept blacks on a lower rung of the economic ladder.

The early civil rights movement found William Holmes Borders, pastor of Wheat Street Baptist Church in the forefront fighting for justice for his people. Samuel Woodrow Williams, a forthright, concerned and courageous, civil rights leader who pastored Friendship Baptist Church and was a former teacher of Martin Luther King, Jr., when he studied at Morehouse College, stood tall among the civil rights leaders of the sixties.

The political awakening is further reflected in the role played by Congressman Andrew Young, who is a member of the historic First Church. Congressman Young served as the executive secretary of the Southern Christian Leadership Conference, founded by Martin Luther King, Jr. He was the constant companion and organizer of many of the nonviolent protest movements during the King era.

Ralph David Abernathy, pastor of West Hunter Baptist Church in Atlanta, has led West Hunter into the mainstream of political and civic awareness. Abernathy was a close associate of King, and succeeded him as president of the Southern Christian Leadership Conference. He is listed as one of the top-ranking influential black leaders in this country.

Martin Luther King, Sr., a strong supporter of his son and a civil rights activist himself, has continued to preach to his congregation at Ebenezer and to the city of Atlanta the doctrine of nonviolent protest as advocated by his son, Martin, Jr.

"Daddy" King, as he is affectionately called, is a part of every political and civic activity in Atlanta. It is rightly believed that the black church has represented the voice of the people and has fostered the spirit of protest in the downtrodden. Out of this black church, a grass roots democracy has emerged which has created a new era of influence in the church and in the political life in the community, which is vital if the black community is to have its rightful place in the social spectrum.

NOTES

CHAPTER I

1. Noel P. Gist and L. A. Halbert, *Urban Society* (New York: 1950), p. 451.

2. Thomas F. Hoult, "Economic Class Consciousness in American Protestantism," *American Sociological Review* 15 (1950): 97.

3. William P. Shriver, *Interchurch World Survey,* American volume p. 31, cited by H. Paul Douglass, *1000 City Churches,* (New York: George H. Doran Co., 1926), p. 249.

4. St. Clair Drake and Horace Cayton, *Black Metropolis* (New York: Harcourt, Brace and Co., 1945), p. 539.

5. See chapter 3, below.

6. Information given by Mrs. J. B. Greenwood, historian of First Church.

7. Gist and Halbert, *Urban Society,* p. 98.

8. U.S. Bureau of the Census, *Sixteenth Census of the United States: 1940. Population and Housing.* (Washington: U.S. Government Printing Office, 1942), pp. 46–48.

9. C.f. *The Social and Economic Pattern of Atlanta, Georgia* (Atlanta: 1939), pp. 63–69.

10. Bruce Barton, *The Church That Saved A City* (Boston: 1914), p. 1.

11. Ibid., p. 4.

12. The scale was developed by the Department of Sociology of Atlanta University in 1950 and used as an instrument for rating areas in the Atlanta Post Screen-test health survey.

13. Douglass, *1000 City Churches,* p. 249.

14. Federal Council of Churches of Christ in America, *Information Service* 39 (No. 3, January 21, 1950): 1–8, cited in T. Lynn Smith and C. A. McMahan, *The Sociology of Urban Life* (New York: Dryden Press, 1951), p. 519.

15. Logan Wilson and William L. Kolb, *Sociological Analysis* (New York: Barnes and Noble Publishers, 1949), p. 395.

16. Everett C. Hughes, "Institutions," in *An Outline of the Principles of Sociology,* edited by Robert E. Park (New York: Barnes and Noble Publishers, 1946), p. 315.

17. Ibid., p. 316.

18. Kimball Young, *Sociology: A Study of Society and Culture* (New York: American Book Co., 1949), p. 375.

19. Gist and Halbert, *Urban Society,* p. 454.

20. Paul H. Landis, *Our Changing Society* (New York: Ginn and Company, 1942), p. 126.

CHAPTER II

1. The census tract boundaries used here are those established for Atlanta at the 1930 census.

2. Tract F–28 includes Baker Street from Courtland Street to Fort Street; Fort Street to Highland Avenue; Highland Avenue to Jackson Street; Jackson Street to Edgewood Avenue; Edgewood Avenue to Courtland Street; and Courtland Street to Baker Street.

3. Tract F–29 includes Highland Avenue from Jackson Street to Southern Railroad; Southern Railroad to Edgewood Avenue; Edgewood Avenue to Jackson Street; and Jackson Street to Highland Avenue.

4. Tract F–36 includes Hunter Street from Vine Street to Davis Street; Davis Street to Mitchell Street; Mitchell Street to Elliott Street; Elliott Street to Nelson Street; Nelson Street to Walker Street; Walker Street to Fair Street; Fair Street to Walnut Street; Walnut Street to Tatnall Street; and Tatnall Street to Hunter Street.

5. Tract F–18 includes North Avenue from Piedmont Avenue to Parkway Drive; Parkway Drive to Highland Avenue; Highland Avenue to Fort Street; Fort Street to Baker; Baker to Courtland; Courtland Street to Currier Street; Currier Street to Piedmont Avenue; and Piedmont Avenue to North Avenue.

6. Tract F–25 includes Simpson Street from Ashby Street to Vine Street; Vine Street to Hunter Street; Hunter Street to Ashby Street; and Ashby Street to Simpson Street.

7. Tract F–43 includes Greensferry Avenue from Ashby Street to Humphries Street; Humphries Street to Liberty Street; Liberty Street to Holland Street; Holland Street to Chapel Street; Chapel Street to Fair Street; Fair Street to Central of Georgia Railroad; Central of Georgia Railroad to Park Street; Park Street to Hammond Street; Hammond Street to South Lawn Street; South Lawn Street to North Lawn Street; North Lawn Street to West-End Avenue; West-

End Avenue to Ashby Street; and Ashby Street to Greensferry Street.

8. Tract F–55 includes Georgia Avenue from Capitol Avenue to Primrose Street; Primrose Street to Atlanta Avenue; Atlanta Avenue to Hill Street; Hill Street to McDonough Boulevard, McDonough Boulevard to Blashfield Street; Blashfield Street to Atlanta City Limits; Atlanta City Limits to Capitol Avenue extended; Capitol Avenue extended to Capitol Avenue; and Capitol Avenue to Georgia Avenue.

9. Tract F–33 includes Edgewood Avenue from Butler Street to Southern Railroad; Southern Railroad to Georgia Railroad to Butler Street; and Butler Street to Edgewood Avenue.

10. Tract F–27 includes Magnolia Street from Southern Railroad to Cain Street; Cain Street to Courtland Street; Courtland Street to Edgewood Avenue; Edgewood Avenue to Butler Street; Butler Street to Georgia Railroad; and Southern Railroad to Magnolia Street.

11. Tract F–19 includes North Avenue from Williams Street to Piedmont Avenue; Piedmont Avenue to Currier Street; Currier Street to Courtland Street; Courtland Street to Cain Street; Cain Street to Williams Street; Williams Street to Hunnicutt Street; and Williams Street to North Avenue.

12. Tract F–56 includes Bass Street from Windsor Street to Capitol Avenue; Capitol Avenue to Southern Railroad; Southern Railroad to Windsor Street extended; Windsor Street extended to Windsor Street; and Windsor Street to Bass Street.

13. Tract F–22 includes Bankhead Avenue to Travis Street to Southern Railroad; Southern Railroad to Simpson Street; Simpson Street to Elm Street; Elm Street to North Avenue; North Avenue to Travis Street; and Travis Street to Bankhead Avenue.

14. Tract D–6 includes Seaboard Air Line Railroad from Whitefoord Avenue to Rogers Street; Rogers Street to Boulevard Drive; Boulevard Drive to Whitefoord Avenue; and Whitefoord Avenue to Seaboard Air Line Railroad.

15. See notes 2 and 3, above, for boundaries of tracts F–28 and F–29.

16. Tract F–26 includes Simpson Street from Vine Street to Elliott Street; Elliott Street to Mitchell Street; Mitchell Street to Davis Street; Davis Street to Hunter Street; Hunter Street to Vine Street; and Vine Street to Simpson Street.

17. See notes 5, 6, 9, 10, and 4, above, for boundaries of tracts F–18, F–25, F–33, F–27, and F–36, respectively.

18. Tract F–42 includes Sells Avenue from Lawton Street to Ashby Street; Ashby Street to West-End Avenue; West-End Avenue to North Lawn Street; North Lawn Street to South Lawn Street; South Lawn Street to Hammond Street; Hammond Street to Park

Street; Park Street to Central of Georgia Railroad to Gordon Street extended; Gordon Street extended to Gordon Street to Lawton Street; and Lawton Street to Sells Avenue.

19. Boundaries for tracts F–18, F–25, F–28, F–29, F–55, F–33, and F–19 are given in notes 5, 6, 2, 3, 8, 9, and 11, above, respectively.

20. Same as above.

21. Tract F–38 includes Hunter Street from Ashby Street to Tatnall Street; Tatnall Street to Walnut Street; Walnut Street to Fair Street; Fair Street to Chapel Street; Chapel Street to Holland Street; Holland Street to Liberty Street; Liberty Street to Humphries Street; Humphries Street to Greensferry Avenue; Greensferry Avenue to Dora Street; Dora Street to Maner Street; Maner Street to Fair Street; Fair Street to Elm Street; Elm Street to Parsons Street; Parsons Street to Lawshe; Lawshe to Greensferry; Greensferry to Ashby Street; and Ashby Street to Hunter Street.

22. Boundaries for tracts F–28, F–29, F–18, F–25, F–33, F–48, and F–36 appear in notes 2, 3, 5, 6, 9, and 4, respectively.

23. Tract F–24 includes Simpson Street from city limits to Ashby Street; Ashby Street to Hunter Street; Hunter Street to Mozley Drive; Mozley Drive to Chappell Road; Chappell Road to city limits; and city limits to Simpson Street.

24. See area rating map prepared by Department of Sociology, Atlanta University.

25. Tract F–39 includes Hunter Street from L. & N. Railroad to Ashby Street; Ashby Street to Sells Avenue; Sells Avenue to Lawton Street; Lawton Street to West View Drive; West View Drive to L. & N. Railroad; and L. & N. Railroad to Hunter Street.

26. Tract F–40 includes the area from the city limits to Chappell Road; Chappell Road to Mozley Drive; Mozley Drive to Hunter Street; Hunter Street to L. & N. Railroad; L. & N. Railroad to Lucile Avenue; Lucile Avenue to Gordon Street; and Gordon Street to city limits.

27. Tract F–23 includes Bankhead Avenue from city limits to Finley Street; Finley Street to Pelham Street; Pelham Street to Ashby Street; Ashby Street to North Avenue; North Avenue to Paynes Street; Paynes Street to Jett Street; Jett Street to Elm Street; Elm Street to Simpson Street; Simpson Street to city limits; and city limits to Bankhead Avenue.

28. Tract F–34 includes Georgia Railroad from Moore Street to Oakland Avenue; Oakland Avenue to Fair Street; Fair Street to Moore Street; and Moore Street to Georgia Railroad.

29. See preceding sections on Residential Patterns for census tract boundaries.

30. See note 16, above, for boundaries of tract F–26.

31. Tract F–17 includes North Avenue from Parkway Drive to North Avenue from Southern Railroad; Southern Railroad to Highland Avenue; Highland Avenue to Parkway Drive; and Parkway Drive to North Avenue.

32. Tract F–37 includes Parson Street from Lawshe Street to Elm Street; Elm Street to Fair Street; Fair Street to Maner Street; Maner Street to Dora Street; Dora Street to Greensferry Avenue; Greensferry Avenue to Lawshe Street; and Lawshe Street to Lawson Street.

33. Tract F–63 includes Mary Street from Stewart Avenue to Mary Street extended to Southern Railroad; Southern Railroad to A. & W. P. Railroad Belt Line to Stewart Avenue; and Stewart Avenue to Mary Street.

34. Tract F–16 includes North Avenue extended to North Avenue from Southern Railroad to Moreland Avenue; Moreland Avenue to Euclid Avenue; Euclid Avenue to Washita Avenue; Washita Avenue to North Highland Avenue; North Highland Avenue to Southern Railroad; and Southern Railroad to North Avenue.

35. Tract F–35 includes Southern Railroad from Elliott Street to Georgia Railroad; Georgia Railroad to Moore Street; Moore Street to Fair Street; Fair Street to Walker Street; Walker Street to Nelson Street; and Nelson Street to Elliott Street.

36. See note 10, above, for boundaries of tract F–27.

37. Tract F–47 includes Fulton Street from Capitol Avenue to Martin Street; Martin Street to Fulton Street; Fulton Street to Connally Street; Connally Street to Glenwood Avenue; Glenwood Avenue to Kelly Street; Kelly Street to Glenn Street; Glenn Street to Primrose Street; Primrose Street to Georgia Avenue; Georgia Avenue to Capitol Avenue; and Capitol Avenue to Fulton Street.

38. Cf., *The Social and Economic Pattern of Atlanta, Georgia.*

39. See note 18, above, for description of tract F–42.

40. Tract F–57 includes Richardson Street from Windsor Street to Capitol Avenue; Capitol Avenue to Bass Street; Bass Street to Windsor Street; and Windsor Street to Richardson Street.

41. Tract F-46 includes Richardson Street from Windsor to Capitol Ave:, Capitol Ave. to Bass St:, Bass Street to Windsor St:, Windsor St. to Richardson St.

42. Tract F-7 includes city limits (Southern Railroad) to Ashby Street extended; Ashby Street extended to Ashby Street to Pelham Street; Pelham Street to Finley Street; Finley Street to Bankhead Avenue; Bankhead Avenue to city limits; and city limits to city limits (Southern Railroad).

43. Tract F-8 includes city limits from Ashby Street to Southern

Railroad; Southern Railroad to Bankhead Avenue; Bankhead Avenue to Travis Street; Travis Street to North Avenue; North Avenue to Elm Street; Elm Street to Jett Street; Jett Street to Paynes Avenue; Paynes Avenue to North Avenue; North Avenue to Ashby Street; and Ashby Street to city limits.

CHAPTER IV

1. Edward Arthur Balridge, "Some Factors Related to Membership and Participation in an Urban Protestant Church," an unpublished master's thesis in the Department of Sociology, Atlanta University, 1953.

BIBLIOGRAPHY

BOOKS

Atkins, Gaius Glenn, and Fagley, Frederick L. *History of American Congregationalism.* Boston: The Pilgrim Press, 1942.

Becker, Howard. "Four Types of Religious Organizations." In *Sociological Analysis.* Edited by L. Wilson and W. L. Kolb. New York: Harcourt, Brace and Company, 1949.

Brownlee, Fred L. *New Day Ascending.* Boston: The Pilgrim Press, 1946.

Buckham, John Wright. *Congregational Churches in the United States.* New York: Houghton Mifflin Company, 1919.

Cuber, John F. "Marginal Church Participants." In *Sociological Analysis.* Edited by L. Wilson and W. L. Kolb. New York: Harcourt, Brace and Co., 1949.

Drake, St. Clair. *Churches and Voluntary Associations in the Chicago Negro Community.* Conducted under the auspices of the Works Progress Administration, Chicago, 1940.

————, and Cayton, Horace. *Black Metropolis.* New York: Harcourt, Brace and Co., 1945.

Douglass, H. Paul. *1000 City Churches.* New York: George H. Doran Co., 1926.

Dubois, W. E. B. *The Negro Church.* Atlanta: Atlanta University Press, 1903.

Dunning, Albert Elijah. *Congregational Churches in the United States.* New York: J. A. Hill and Co., 1894.

Edwards, Jonathan. *Congregational Churches.* New York: American Book Co., 1935.

Fauset, Arthur Huff. *Black Gods of the Metropolis.* Philadelphia: Pennsylvania Press, 1944.

Frazier, E. Franklin. *The Negro Family in the United States.* Chicago: University of Chicago Press, 1946.

Landis, Paul H. *Our Changing Society.* New York: Ginn and Company, 1942.

Latourette, Kenneth S. et al. *Church and Community.* New York: Willett, Clark and Company, 1938.

Loescher, Frank S. *The Protestant Church and the Negro.* New York: Association Press, 1948.

May, Henry Farnham. *Protestant Churches in Industrial America.* New York: Harper and Co., 1949.

Mays, Benjamin, and Nicholson, Joseph William. *The Negro's Church.* New York: Institute of Social and Religious Research, 1933.

Myrdal, Gunnar. *An American Dilemma.* New York: Harper and Brothers, 1944.

Nelson, Wm. Stuart. *Church and Social Problems—U.S.* New York: Harpers, 1948.

Odum, Howard W. *American Sociology.* New York: Longmans, Green and Co., 1951.

Pope, Liston. "Patterns of Denominational Development: Churches and Sects." In *Sociological Analysis.* Edited by L. Wilson and W. L. Kolb. New York: Harcourt, Brace and Co., 1949.

Richardson, Harry V. *Dark Glory.* New York: Friendship Press, 1947.

Smith, Lynn T., and McMahan, C. A. *The Sociology of Urban Life.* New York: Dryden Press, 1951.

The Social and Economic Pattern of Atlanta, Georgia. A Report prepared by Works Progress Administration of Atlanta, Georgia, 1939.

U.S. Bureau of the Census. 1950. *Housing, V.* Washington: U.S. Government Printing Office, 1952.

U.S. Bureau of Census. Sixteenth Census of the United States: 1940. *Population and Housing.* Washington: U.S. Government Printing Office, 1942.

Warner, W. Lloyd, et al. *Democracy in Jonesville.* New York: Harper and Brothers, 1949.

Woodson, Carter Godwin. *The History of the Negro Church.* Washington: The Associated Publishers, 1921.

Young, Kimball. *Sociology—A Study of Society and Culture.* New York: American Book Company, 1949.

ARTICLES

Hoult, Thomas F. "Economic Class Consciousness in American Protestantism." *American Sociological Review* 15 (1950): 97.

Hughes, Everett C. "Institutions." In *New Outline of the Principles of Sociology.* Edited by Alfred McClung Lee. New York: Barnes and Noble Inc., 1943.

————. "The Ecological Aspects of Institutions." *American Sociological Review* 1 (1938): 180.

Johnson, Guy B. "Some Factors in the Development of Negro Social Institutions in the United States." *American Journal of Sociology* 40 (1934): 329.

Mukerjee, Radhakarnal. "Ecological and Cultural Patterns of Social Organizations." *American Sociological Review* 8 (1943): 643.

UNPUBLISHED MATERIAL

Balridge, Edward Arthur. "Some Factors Related to Membership and Participation in an Urban Protestant Church." Unpublished manuscript, Department of Sociology, Atlanta University, 1953.

Wright, John C. "Facts and Figures Concerning the First Congregational Church." Unpublished booklet prepared by the pastor, December, 1941.